Contents

KT-226-132

Electrical goods

The modern world depends on electricity. Each day we use all sorts of electrical appliances, many of which are essential to a 21st-century way of life.

All sorts of electrical gadgets

Modern homes are full of electrical appliances. Kitchens have microwaves, fridges, freezers, washing machines and dishwashers. There are electric mixers, juicers and much more. Elsewhere in the home there are televisions with satellite boxes, computers, DVD players, games consoles and MP3 players.

Many people entertain themselves by watching television or playing on games consoles.

OLD ELECTRICAL GOODS

Sally Morgan

W

FRANKLIN WATTS
LONDON • SYDNEY

First published in 2006 by Franklin Watts
338 Euston Road,
London NW1 3BH

Franklin Watts Australia
Hachette Children's Books
Level 17/207 Kent Street,
Sydney NSW 2000

Produced for Franklin Watts by White-Thomson Publishing Ltd
210 High Street,
Lewes BN7 2NH

Editor: Rachel Minay
Designer: Brenda Cole
Picture research: Morgan Interactive Ltd
Consultant: Graham Williams

Picture credits
The publishers would like to thank the following for reproducing these photographs:
Alamy 6 (Janine Wiedel); Ecoscene front cover main image (Ray Roberts), front cover
top right (Tony Page), 8 (Sally Morgan), 9 (Tony Page), 10 (Ray Roberts), 11, 12, 13
(Ceanne Jansen), 14, 15 (Angela Hampton), 16 (Lorenzo Lees), 17 (Mark Caney), 18
(Angela Hampton), 20 (Melanie Peters), 21 (Tony Page), 22 (Pete Cairns), 23 (Ceanne
Jansen), 24 (Sally Morgan), 25 (Stuart Donachie), 26 (Ray Roberts), 27 (Angela
Hampton); Imagestate 7 (Robert Llewellyn); NASA 19; Recyclenow.com front cover
bottom right.

Every attempt has been made to clear copyright. Should there be
any inadvertent omission please apply to the publisher for rectification.

British Library Cataloguing in Publication Data
A CIP catalogue record for this book
is available from the British Library.

ISBN-10: 0 7496 6437 1
ISBN-13: 978 0 7496 6437 4

Dewey classification: 363.72'88

Printed in China

It's my world!

People use many electrical items in their daily lives. Make a record of all the different ones that you use in one day. Which ones are essential and which ones could you do without?

Schools in the developed world, such as this one in the USA, are well equipped with computers so that each pupil in a class has access to one.

Using raw materials

Each year the number of electrical appliances made throughout the world increases and this uses up raw materials. Then the appliances are packaged and transported to shops to be sold to consumers. When they are put into use they use up electricity.

More waste

People create a lot of waste, including paper, glass, plastic and garden clippings. The fastest growing type of waste is electrical waste. At the end of their lives, many electrical appliances are dumped with the rubbish. This is a loss of valuable materials that could be recycled.

Making waste

Each year people throw away huge quantities of electrical waste including old televisions, fridges, computers and mobile phones. This may be because they no longer work or simply because they have been replaced by newer models. Much of this waste ends up in huge holes in the ground called landfills, but lots of it could be recycled instead.

All sorts of electrical goods have been put in this skip for recycling. The metal parts are valuable and can be recycled over and over again.

Cost of repair

In the past it was common to keep electrical appliances for a long time. This was partly because electrical appliances were more expensive to buy, compared with earnings. Also, electrical appliances were well made and they could be taken apart and repaired. Now it is often cheaper to throw something away and buy a new one. Many of the less expensive appliances are not designed to be repaired. For example, if an iron is dropped on the floor the plastic may crack. This is difficult to repair so there is no alternative but to replace it.

Keeping up to date

Some electrical appliances are replaced even when they are in perfect working order because they are no longer fashionable. For example, new models of mobile phones and games consoles are produced and for some people it is important to have the latest model.

It's my world!

Have a look at the electrical appliances in your home. How many are more than five years old? How many are less than one year old?

Did you know...?

Electronic and electrical equipment makes up on average 4% of European domestic waste, and this amount is growing three times faster than any other type of waste.

Business waste

Businesses create a lot of electrical waste, too, especially computers. Computers are getting faster and more powerful all the time, so within a couple of years a computer or monitor can be out of date. For example, people are replacing the old bulky monitors – even though there is nothing wrong with them – with the latest flat-screen monitors because they take up less space on a desk.

This huge pile of old fridges and freezers is waiting to be recycled.

Reusing computers

The average life of a computer is just three years and it is likely that this will fall within the next few years to just one to two years. It is estimated that for every new computer that is purchased, another is thrown away. Nine out of every ten of these computers are in perfect working order.

Second-hand computers

Computers do not need to be dumped. Computers that are in working order can be sold to other people or taken to shops that sell second-hand computers and accessories such as printers, CD writers, hard drives and monitors. Also, there are companies that specialize in taking older computers and bringing them up to date by giving them faster processors or more memory.

It's my world!

Do you use a computer at school? Computers are an essential part of modern learning, but imagine what it would be like if your school did not have a computer. Find out what happens to the computers in your school when they are no longer required.

This computer workshop collects old computers. They are checked and repaired so they can be used again.

This warehouse is full of old computer monitors. Some will be sold but others will be taken apart and recycled.

Computer aid

A business may not want a computer that is more than a few years old, but there are plenty of people in the world who would like to have the opportunity to own a computer. In many developing countries 99 people out of every 100 do not have a computer and most schools lack computers, too. There are charities that specialize in supplying computers to people in developing countries. Businesses can give their old computers to these charities who will check that the computers are in perfect working order before shipping them overseas.

Recycling computers

Although a few computers are reused, most are thrown away. In the past, computers and all the bits that go with them, such as printers, scanners and cables, ended up in landfill sites. This is changing as governments pass laws that require the manufacturers to take back computers at the end of their lives.

Valuable metals

Computers may look as if they are made mostly of plastic but there is a significant amount of metal inside the circuit board and hard drives. An old-style computer monitor and circuit boards together contain about 3 kilograms of lead, which is valuable, but also harmful. In addition, there are smaller amounts of gold, mercury, cadmium, copper, chromium and arsenic, many of which are also harmful. Computers have to be taken apart and recycled carefully to make sure the harmful materials do not leak out or even poison the person doing the recycling. The plastic cases can be recycled, too.

These connectors contain plastic and metal, which can be extracted and recycled.

These computer circuit boards have been cut up and made into clipboards and key rings.

It's my world!

More than 375 million printer cartridges are thrown away each year worldwide. What do you do with the old cartridges from a printer? When you open the packaging for a cartridge, check inside to see if there are any instructions about recycling it. Some companies provide a postage-paid envelope in which you can send the cartridge for recycling. Some organisations collect used cartridges and raise money for charity. Sometimes you can take your old cartridge to a shop to be refilled.

Recycling cartridges

A printer cartridge is mostly plastic and aluminium, which can be recycled. The large toner cartridges for a laser printer or a photocopier can be reused. They are completely dismantled and cleaned, any worn parts are replaced, and the drum is either re-coated or replaced. They are then refilled with fresh toner, tested and sold with a guarantee.

Mobile phones

The number of mobile phones in the world is increasing rapidly. In 2005, an estimated 780 million mobile phones were sold around the world. This creates a lot of potential waste for the future.

Hazardous materials

Mobile phones contain metals such as platinum, gold, silver and copper, and hazardous materials such as cadmium. These materials are completely harmless in the phone, but if they are dumped into a landfill they can leak into the ground and pollute water sources. For example, the cadmium from one mobile phone battery is enough to pollute 600,000 litres of water. Therefore, mobile phones have to be disposed of safely rather than thrown away. Shops that sell mobile phones have collection points for old phones. Some allow you to trade in your old phone when you buy a new one.

Having the latest model of mobile phone can be important to some people and they replace their phones regularly.

Did you know...?

Old mobile phones can be valuable. There are schemes that raise money for charity by recycling mobile phones. See if your school could start a mobile phone collection scheme and raise money for new equipment or for a local charity.

Many mobile phone shops collect old mobile phones and send them to be recycled.

Recycling a phone

Any mobile phones that are in good condition can be sent to developing countries to be reused. They may not be the latest models but they work well. Older models have to be recycled. The phones are taken apart and the battery is recycled separately (see page 17). The plastic casing is removed and broken up into small crumbs called granules. These can be sent to manufacturers that use recycled plastic. The plastic from mobile phones can be put to lots of uses, such as making traffic cones and artificial surfaces for playgrounds and sports facilities. The metal parts can also be melted down and recycled.

Batteries

Batteries are used to power items such as laptop computers, mobile phones, clocks, toys, cameras and much more. These kinds of items use dry-cell batteries. They are small and convenient but each year millions are thrown away.

The dry batteries that are used to power toys, games consoles and other electrical items have to be replaced regularly.

Types of battery

There are different types of dry-cell battery. Most batteries are of the type that is used once and thrown away. They contain chemicals such as zinc chloride, mercuric oxide or silver oxide. Another type of battery is the rechargeable battery, which can be used over and over again because it can be recharged using electricity. These batteries contain chemicals such as nickel, cadmium or lithium. It is better to use rechargeable batteries as this reduces the number of batteries that need to be bought and then thrown away.

Did you know...?

▸ Each year, Americans buy about 3.5 billion batteries – that works out at about 32 batteries per family. Australians discard about 8,000 tonnes of used batteries each year.

▸ The energy needed to make a battery is 50 times greater than the energy it gives out.

Recycling batteries

Batteries should be recycled rather than put in the bin. Sometimes there are special recycling points for batteries. The different types have to be recycled separately because they contain different chemicals, some of which, for example cadmium and mercury, are harmful. The metal that forms the case of the battery can also be recycled. Most batteries are recycled by heating, which causes the metal to melt and separate out. The metals can then be made into new batteries or other items.

It's my world!

What can you do?

- Use mains electricity when possible rather than a battery.

- Use rechargeable batteries and a battery charger.

- Try to use rechargers that are powered from a small solar panel or from a wind-up mechanism, for example there are some wind-up mobile phone chargers.

- Dispose of all your batteries safely by taking them to battery recycling points.

- Send batteries back to manufacturers for recycling or reprocessing if a scheme is available.

Dangerous waste

If batteries end up in landfill sites they may start to leak. The chemicals seep out into the ground and may be carried by water into local streams. This can poison fish and other aquatic animals.

This dry battery has ended up on the seabed. The chemicals in the battery will leak out into the water and could harm nearby marine life.

Fridges and freezers

A fridge is an essential piece of equipment in the kitchen as it keeps food fresh for longer. In recent years the number of fridges and freezers in the world has increased as more people can afford to buy them. There are very few homes in Australia, Europe or North America without a fridge or freezer.

Inside a fridge

Fridges and freezers have an outer casing made of metal or plastic and an insulating wall of foam. The inside is covered in plastic so it can be wiped down. All fridges and freezers contain a coolant. This is a liquid that circulates within the appliance. It keeps the inside cool by taking heat from the inside and releasing it to the outside.

A lot of raw materials are used to make a large fridge including metals, plastic and coolant. These can all be recycled.

It's my world!

A fridge uses electricity to stay cool. There are ways to minimize the use of electricity. Fridges should never be placed near an oven as the heat from the oven causes the fridge to work much harder. Check the temperature setting of the fridge. There is no need to have it on the coldest setting unless the weather is very warm. Do not keep opening the fridge as cool air escapes each time. Also, do not place hot foods in the fridge. Leave them on the side until they have cooled down.

CFCs

In the past, the coolant used in fridges was a chemical called CFC or chloroflurocarbon. This chemical was used widely in all forms of refrigeration equipment, fire extinguishers, air conditioning units and aerosols. It was also used in the foam lining of fridges. Then it was discovered that CFCs were destroying ozone high in the atmosphere. Ozone is important because it absorbs harmful ultraviolet light in sunlight. The ozone had to be protected, so during the 1990s most countries banned the manufacture of CFCs and related chemicals. More recently it has been discovered that CFCs are also greenhouse gases and they contribute to global warming. There are many fridges and freezers that contain CFCs still in existence and they have to be disposed of carefully.

The ozone layer is thinning over Antarctica. The levels of ozone have been measured and this photo shows the results. The dark blue area shows where the ozone layer is thinnest.

Reusing and recycling fridges

Some unwanted fridges and freezers can be reused. There are companies that take old appliances and refurbish them so that they can be resold. They drain out any CFCs and replace them with a safe alternative. Then they check that the appliance works and resell it.

Second-hand use

New fridges and freezers are expensive in many developing countries and people cannot afford to buy them. As a result, there is a trade in second-hand fridges and freezers from developed countries. The CFCs are removed by specialist refrigeration companies and replaced with a different coolant before the fridge or freezer is exported.

In some countries, fridges that no longer work are taken apart and the spare parts used to repair other fridges.

Does it contain CFCs?

Most fridges are marked with an 'appliance rating plate'. This is a metal plate or sticky label on the back of the appliance. The plate contains information about the appliance, for example model and serial number and the type of coolant it uses. Fridges that are marked with R12 or R134a on the plate will probably have CFCs or HCFC in the insulation foam, which will need special treatment when the fridge is recycled.

Did you know...?

As many as 3 million domestic fridges and freezers are disposed of each year in the UK. Of these, 90% are recycled.

The metal casing of a fridge is shredded and poured into bags. This makes it easier to transport the metal to factories where it will be recycled.

The recycling process

In some countries, for example in Japan, and the European Union, laws prevent fridges and freezers from being dumped in landfills. If a fridge or freezer cannot be repaired it must be recycled. About 90% of a fridge can be recycled. The CFCs are drained out and usually burnt. Any CFCs in the foam insulation are also removed and burnt. Then the external case and things like shelves are stripped out.

This leaves a white box, which is shredded. The bags of shredded fridges contain different materials, such as metal and different plastics, which are separated and recycled. The plastics can be sent to factories that make new goods – such as plant pots, boots and garden furniture – from recycled plastic. Metals can be melted down and shaped into a wide range of new objects.

Electric lights

Homes are lit up by a variety of light bulbs such as tungsten lights, low-energy bulbs and fluorescent tubes. There are lots of lights on streets, too. When they come to the end of their lives they are thrown away. Fluorescent tubes in particular need to be disposed of carefully because they contain mercury, a poisonous chemical.

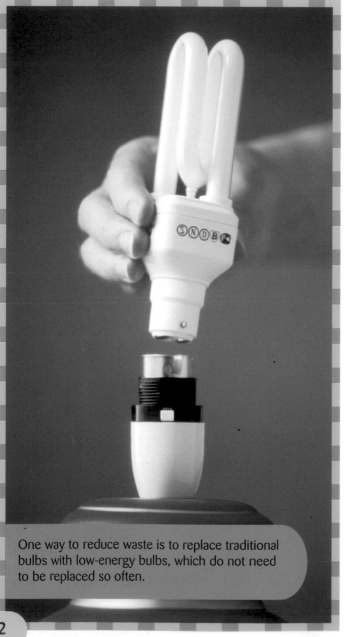

One way to reduce waste is to replace traditional bulbs with low-energy bulbs, which do not need to be replaced so often.

It's my world!

Have a look at the electrical lights in your home. You may be surprised by how many there are. Are any of them fluorescent lights? Do you know if there are any low-energy bulbs? How could you reduce the amount of electricity that is used by lights in your home?

Low-energy bulbs

Tungsten filament bulbs used in the home have to be replaced regularly and most end up in the bin. These bulbs are not usually recycled although the metals inside could be melted down. A better alternative is to use a long-lasting low-energy bulb. Not only do these bulbs use far less electricity, they last longer, so fewer need to be thrown away.

Did you know...?

As many as 500 million fluorescent lamps are dumped in landfills in the USA every year. These lamps may contain as much as four tonnes of mercury. Mercury is so dangerous that the mercury from one fluorescent tube can pollute 30,000 litres of water beyond a safe level for drinking.

Fluorescent tubes

Fluorescent tubes can be recycled. The tubes are taken to a recycling facility where the main components of glass, metal and mercury are separated. The tube has to be taken apart carefully to make sure the mercury vapour does not escape.

This man is wearing protective clothing and breathing apparatus because he is taking old fluorescent tubes apart and they contain mercury. He is pushing the tube into a machine that removes the mercury vapour.

Recycling packaging

Electrical goods are sold surrounded by lots of packaging. A new fridge for example is packed in polystyrene foam and wrapped in plastic inside a cardboard case. This packaging is needed to protect the goods during transportation but it should not be thrown away as much of it can be recycled.

Recycling cardboard

Cardboard can be shredded, mixed with water and stirred until it breaks down into individual fibres. Foreign objects, such as staples and bits of tape, are removed using filters. The clean pulp is passed through a series of rollers. This flattens it and removes any remaining water.

Making cardboard from recycled pulp uses about 75% of the energy used in the manufacture of cardboard from new pulp. However, each time cardboard is recycled, the fibres become weaker limiting the number of times it can be recycled. This is usually about eight times. To avoid this, the recycled pulp is often mixed with new pulp. Cardboard can also be recycled to make chipboard, paperboard (flat card used to make cereal boxes etc.), paper towels, tissues, newsprint and writing paper.

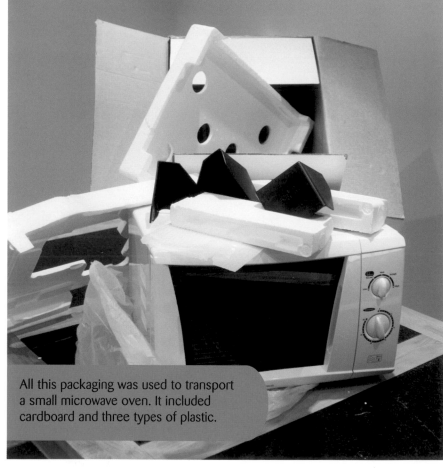

All this packaging was used to transport a small microwave oven. It included cardboard and three types of plastic.

These cardboard boxes have been collected for recycling from a market in this Chinese town.

It's my world!

Next time your family buys an electrical appliance make sure that as much of the packaging as possible is recycled. Cardboard can usually be taken to local recycling centres. Look to see if the cardboard is made from recycled material already. This will be indicated by a triangular recycling symbol with a number in the middle that represents the percentage of recycled paper. Some recycling centres take polystyrene packaging, too.

Polystyrene

The polystyrene foam can be recycled, too. Polystyrene is identified by a symbol stamped onto its surface. It is a triangle with the number 6 in the middle. Polystyrene is taken to factories where it is washed, flaked, dried and squeezed into recycled polystyrene pellets. The pellets are melted down and made into new polystyrene objects.

The way ahead

There are many ways of tackling the problem of increasing electrical waste. They include extending the life of the product, making it more energy efficient so it uses less electricity, and encouraging more recycling.

Longer product life

If electrical appliances had a longer life people would not have to buy so many. One way forward could be for manufacturers to extend the warranty period. This is the period during which the manufacturer repairs the appliance free of charge. It has been proved that extended warranty periods encourage consumers to keep an appliance for longer. Electrical appliances also need to be easy to dismantle and repair. This can be improved at the design stage of the product.

This sculpture is made from 3 tonnes of electrical waste. It includes 5 fridges, 35 mobile phones, 5 sandwich toasters and 4 lawnmowers. Its teeth are made from computer mice, its spine from a washing machine and neck from a vacuum cleaner.

Using less electricity

Electrical appliances use up a lot of electricity and most electricity is generated using coal, oil or gas. These fuels create polluting gases when they are burnt. An energy-efficient appliance is one that is designed to carry out its job using the minimum amount of electricity. If people bought energy-efficient appliances and fitted low-energy light bulbs, the demand for electricity would reduce. It would be even better if the electricity was generated using renewable energy, such as the sun or wind.

Recycling everything

The amount of electrical waste can be reduced if everybody makes sure that all old electrical appliances, batteries and printer cartridges are recycled.

It's my world!

What can you do?

▸ Turn off electric appliances such as televisions, computers and lights when they are not in use to save electricity. Many people leave televisions, DVDs and computers on 'standby' but this just wastes electricity.

▸ Use rechargeable batteries.

▸ Try to keep mobile phones, games consoles and similar items for as long as possible. When you decide to upgrade, make sure the old one is handed on to somebody else or recycled.

▸ Recycle all the packaging that comes with a new electrical appliance.

Turn off lights and electrical goods when they are not in use.

Glossary

Appliance
a household device operated by electricity or gas

Battery
a device that stores electricity

CFC (chloroflurocarbon)
a chemical used in refrigeration that is harmful to the ozone layer

Coolant
a fluid that is used to carry heat away from something

Developed country
a country in which most people have a high standard of living

Developing country
a country in which most people have a low standard of living and who have poor access to goods and services compared with people in a developed country

Efficiency
a measure of how much energy something uses in order to carry out its function, for example an energy-efficient fridge will use less electricity to keep food chilled than a less efficient fridge

Global warming
the gradual warming of the average temperature of the Earth, caused by an increase in greenhouse gases

Greenhouse gas
a gas in the atmosphere that traps heat

Landfill
a large hole in the ground used to dispose of waste

Ozone layer
a layer high in the Earth's atmosphere that contains the gas ozone (a form of oxygen) and absorbs harmful ultraviolet light from the sun

Pollute
to release harmful materials into the environment

Recycle
to process and reuse materials in order to make new items

Reduce
to lower the amount of waste produced

Reuse
to use something again, either in the same way or in a different way

Tungsten
a chemical element, used to make electric light filaments

Waste
anything that is thrown away, abandoned, or released into the environment in a way that could harm the environment

Websites

Freecycle
www.freecycle.com
Website where members can send emails to other members of the group listing items that they want to recycle free of charge rather than dumping them on a landfill site.

Friendly Packaging
http://friendlypackaging.org.uk/novel.htm
Website about the different types of materials that are used in packaging and how they can be recycled.

Friends of the Earth
www.foe.org.uk
Website of the charity Friends of the Earth that gives information about campaigns, including those for encouraging recycling and against incinerators and landfills.

Let's Recycle
www.letsrecycle.com/index.jsp
Website looking at all sorts of waste and how it can be recycled.

London Remade
www.londonremade.com/index.asp
Website looking at the different recycling schemes in London and how people can recycle more.

Recycling near you
www.recyclingnearyou.com.au/
A useful Australian website to find out what you can recycle in your local area.

United States Environmental Protection Agency
www.epa.gov
This website has lots of environmental information on all issues, not just waste. There is an EPA Kids Club (www.epa.gov/kids) with information on waste and recycling.

Waste Online
www.wasteonline.org.uk
Comprehensive website looking at all aspects of recycling.

Waste Wise
www.wastewise.wa.gov.au/pages/recycling.asp
An Australian website with information about how to recycle anything and everything.

Every effort has been made by the publisher to ensure that these websites are suitable for children and contain no inappropriate or offensive material. However, because of the nature of the internet it is impossible to guarantee that the contents of these sites will not be altered. We strongly advise that internet access is supervised by a responsible adult.

Index